I0692595

Robert Warington

Some of the principles which should determine

compensation for the use of foods and manures

A lecture delivered before the Newcastle Farmers' Club on February 26,

1898

Robert Warington

Some of the principles which should determine compensation for the use of foods and manures
A lecture delivered before the Newcastle Farmers' Club on February 26, 1898

ISBN/EAN: 9783337200947

Printed in Europe, USA, Canada, Australia, Japan

Cover: Foto ©Andreas Hilbeck / pixelio.de

More available books at **www.hansebooks.com**

SOME OF THE PRINCIPLES

WHICH SHOULD DETERMINE

COMPENSATION

FOR THE USE OF

FOODS AND MANURES

A LECTURE

DELIVERED BEFORE THE NEWCASTLE FARMERS' CLUB

ON FEBRUARY 26, 1898

BY

ROBERT WARINGTON, M.A., F.R.S.

FORMERLY PROFESSOR OF RURAL ECONOMY IN THE UNIVERSITY OF OXFORD
EXAMINER IN AGRICULTURE TO THE DEPARTMENT OF
SCIENCE AND ART

LONDON

VINTON & CO., 9 NEW BRIDGE STREET, E.C.

1898

PRINTED BY
SPOTTISWOODE AND CO., NEW-STREET SQUARE
LONDON

Some of the Principles which should determine Compensation for the use of Foods and Manures.

THE task which is before me this afternoon is, you know, one of great difficulty. The proper compensation to be given under various circumstances for the use of purchased foods and manures upon a farm is a subject beset with complications. I enjoy, however, a few special advantages. I am addressing an audience which includes men thoroughly familiar with the problems of which I have to treat. It also fortunately happens that the veteran investigators at Rothamsted—Sir J. B. Lawes and Sir J. H. Gilbert—have just given us their latest views on the subject in the Journal of the Royal Agricultural Society, 1897, p. 674, and have republished in a revised form their table showing the calculated manure value of the various foods consumed on the farm, the former estimated values being altered so as to correspond with the present market prices of nitrogen, phosphoric acid, and potash. I am thus relieved from a discussion of one important section of the subject, and am able to give fuller attention to other matters.

My object to-day is to bring before you certain questions which arise from a scientific consideration of the subject, and also to make you acquainted with certain facts, the result of actual experiments, which will help, I think, to inform the valuer's judgment, and enable him to come to a more correct decision upon the questions before him. To suggest a definite scheme of valuations is not my purpose; it would be presumptuous on my part to attempt to do this. Every detailed scheme of valuations must be made by local men, by persons intimately acquainted with the systems of agriculture pursued in the district, and with the results which farmers usually obtain, and especially with the characters of the prevailing soils, and the extent to which they respond to applications of manures, or to other methods of amelioration.

Looking at the question of compensation from the point of view of simple equity, we should, I think, conclude that an outgoing tenant might fairly claim to be compensated for all his unexhausted substantial improvements of the fertility of the land, which are over and above the acts required of him by agreement with his landlord. The farm has been granted by the landlord with certain stipulated conditions as to its cultivation : if the tenant does more for the land than these conditions require, he is entitled to compensation for any unexhausted value of his improvements ; while the landlord, on the other hand, may claim as a set-off any deterioration of fertility arising from the nonfulfilment of the stipulated conditions. According to the Act of 1883, the amount of compensation is to be determined by the value of the improvements to the incoming tenant.

WHAT SHOULD BE RECKONED AN IMPROVEMENT ?

The first question I wish to raise is, What should be held to constitute an improvement ? By an improvement we clearly imply something which is beneficial; in the case before us it must mean some action the consequences of which have a substantial value to the incoming tenant. The Act of Parliament contains a schedule of improvements for the execution of which compensation is to be awarded at the discretion of the referee. Now my point is this, that the actions thus scheduled as improvements are not necessarily in every case productive of substantial benefit, and that all of them in various cases confer benefit in very different degrees. I take it, therefore, that the first aim of a referee under this Act of Parliament should be to ascertain what amount of substantial benefit the successor to the farm will obtain from the so-called improvements made by the outgoing tenant ; this fact, rather than the bills for manures, foods, or work done, should form the basis of the compensation awarded. If great care is not taken on this point we shall soon find ourselves in the meshes of a system of paper valuations representing no substantial value, which will in time become a grievous burden to the agriculturist.

Let me now illustrate what I have said by examples. You will, I think, agree with me that the burning of a clay soil, which is scheduled as an improvement in the Act of Parliament, is an operation which is beneficial only in certain cases, and may, in fact, when unwisely carried out, be productive of much mischief. Liming, again, is another of the scheduled improvements, which, if unwisely performed, may injure instead of benefiting an incoming tenant. The deterioration of fertility due to over-liming is, in fact, well-known in those districts where lime is commonly employed.

Many cases will arise in which applications of manures upon a particular soil leave no result of any substantial value to the succeeding tenant, while on another soil the use of the same manures may constitute a fair claim to compensation. Applications of potash salts furnish us with a good example of this variable effect of manures. There is much land in England on which potash salts are not a paying manure, and not unfrequently their application to arable land produces no appreciable effect. In other parts of England, however, the beneficial effect of potash salts is very marked, and the residue of the manure in the soil is undoubtedly of advantage to the succeeding tenant. Here is a case in which a local valuer, instead of following a hard and fast rule, should be guided by the experience of the district, and award compensation, or withhold it, according to the amount of substantial benefit which the incoming tenant will receive. It is futile to argue that the residue of potash is in every case in the soil, and, therefore, must be of future use; if this future is very distant, and the return in crops extremely slow and uncertain, the benefit can hardly be supposed to have an appreciable money value.

In the example just given we have an instance of the worthlessness of superfluous manure. The land on which the potash produced no effect contained itself enough for the wants of all the crops which it produced, and consequently the supply of more potash was attended with no profit. The case is one of far-reaching importance. I shall have illustrations to give you presently, showing, on the one hand, the very great effect produced by residues of manure on poor land ; and, on the other, the absence of any effect when the land is already in a condition to produce full crops. When the illustrations are before us we shall have to consider the bearing of these facts on the question of compensation.

The behaviour of phosphatic manures furnishes us with another class of illustrations. Bones are often a very valuable manure on light and medium soils, but they are almost without effect when applied to heavy land ; while basic slag gives its best results on clay soils. Finely ground mineral phosphates, if not crystalline in their structure, form effective manures on soils containing little lime, while on calcareous soils their value is very small. In this class of illustrations it is not the poverty or richness of the soils in phosphates which .determines the result, but the varying power of the soils to render phosphates soluble and available as plant food. The special suitability of basic slag to clay soils is probably due to the excess of lime which it contains. In the case of all the phosphates mentioned their physical condition will also have a considerable influence on their effectiveness ; thus half-inch bone and bone-dust will disappear with very different rapidity in the soil, and will require a different scale of compensation. Facts such as I have just mentioned ought clearly to be taken into account by a skilled referee when deciding what compensation should be given for the use of phosphatic manures. Manures which are unsuitable and ineffective must always be treated as of little value to the incoming tenant.

The influence of the physical condition of the soil on the effectiveness of manures is far-reaching. All organic manures, such as farmyard manure, sea-weed, green manures, and shoddy, will be of much greater value when applied to a moderately light, well aerated soil, than when applied to one which is naturally consolidated and wet. The saying that on heavy land tillage is of more importance than manure expresses a great truth, which the professional valuer must take into account as well as the farmer.

The referee will sometimes have further to take into account the kind of crop to which the manure has been applied, and the use to which that crop has been put by the farmer. When nitrate of soda, or sulphate of ammonia, has been applied to the soil, it is generally assumed that no valuable residue of the manure remains in the land to serve as plant food in the following season, and valuers in most cases decline to give any compensation to the outgoing tenant for the nitrate or ammonia salts which he has employed. If these manures have been used to grow crops which the farmer has sold, the valuer is probably right, though we shall see by-and-bye that there may be exceptions to this rule; but if the nitrate or ammonia has been used to grow a crop of mangels or grass, and these crops have been consumed by stock on the farm, the case becomes quite different. A considerable part of the nitrogen of the manure is now transferred to the dung heap, or has been returned in the form of animal manure to the land, and this nitrogen as truly deserves compensation as the nitrogen furnished by the consumption of oil-cake.[1]

If we turn from the artificial manures to the manure obtained from the consumption of purchased foods by stock, we again find that the value of the manure depends greatly on a variety of circumstances, and that it is impossible that a single mode of reckoning should do justice in all cases.

We have first to take into account how much of the nitrogen, phosphates, and potash of the food will be retained by the animal consuming it, and thus never enter the manure. You are aware that in the case of a cow in full milk, or of a young rapidly growing animal, the proportion of these constituents retained may be very considerable; that in the case of a full-

---

[1] The experiments with mangels at Rothamsted show that when these roots are grown on a fairly heavy soil, with a good supply of ash constituents, the proportion of nitrogen assimilated by the crop from a dressing of nitrate of soda is very large. About 60 per cent. of the nitrogen of the nitrate will be found, on an average, in the mangel roots, while a considerable further portion is stored up in the leaves. The quantity of nitrogen, purchased as nitrate of soda, which will be finally returned to the land as animal manure on the consumption of the roots, may thus be considerable. The same return of the nitrogen of the nitrate as animal manure will occur when the nitrate is applied to grass crops consumed on the farm. Nitrates do not apparently increase the produce of leguminous fodder crops, and in their case the present argument does not apply.

grown fattening animal the proportion retained is quite small ; while in the case of a working horse or ox, neither gaining nor losing weight, the amount retained is practically nothing.

We have next to take into account the subsequent treatment of the manure. The losses of nitrogen which may occur from imperfect methods of treatment are very large, amounting to at least one-half of the nitrogen originally present in the fresh liquid and solid excrements. Accurate investigations on the subject are much needed. We may say, however, with some confidence, that the most effective use of foods as manure is obtained when the food is consumed upon the land. When cake is consumed by sheep feeding off turnips on the land ; when the plough follows up the hurdles without delay, and barley is at once sown, we have conditions under which the manure from the cake will yield its best return. Cake consumed on pasture is probably not quite so effective, as the distribution of the manure is in this case far less perfect. If manure is made at the farm buildings, the preparation of the manure in boxes or deep stalls, where it remains undisturbed under the animal, fresh litter being spread on the top each day, is the most perfect method yet adopted. If the manure is daily carried to a heap, the losses of nitrogen at once become very considerable. To diminish loss as far as possible the escape of urine must be carefully prevented, and the manure heap must be kept thoroughly consolidated, and thoroughly moist. When the heap is to be preserved for some time it should be covered with a layer of earth well beaten together.

We have said enough to show how greatly the practical value of every manure will vary under the variety of conditions which occur in agriculture. It is impossible, therefore, to take the mere cost of the manure, or cake, which the outgoing tenant has employed in the latter years of his tenancy, as in itself a sufficient basis for estimating the value of the unexhausted improvements which he leaves on the farm; a number of other considerations must be taken into account before the practical value of these improvements to the succeeding tenant can be determined. The Newcastle Club acted very wisely when in 1884 it arranged its scale of compensation for each manure in three grades, thus allowing more compensation to be awarded in some cases than in others. It is only by working in this manner that real justice can be done to all parties.

LESSONS TAUGHT BY FIELD EXPERIMENTS.

I turn now to the second part of my subject. I want to bring before you, and especially before the valuers who may be present, the results of actual trials in the field, which supply examples of the returns obtainable from the residues of previous manuring, and which show how the value of these residues will vary under different circumstances. One could wish that the facts which must most influence our judgment had been far more numerous, but though few they are worthy of our best attention. The practical results I am about to mention are gathered from the field experiments made at Rothamsted and at Woburn. Unpublished details respecting the Rothamsted experiments have been kindly placed at my disposal by Sir J. B. Lawes and Sir J. H. Gilbert, and respecting the Woburn experiments by Dr. J. A. Voelcker, for the purposes of this lecture.

It is well at starting to remember that the soils at these two stations are very different. At Rothamsted the surface soil is a heavy loam with flint stones; the subsoil is usually clay; at a considerable distance from the surface is the chalk, which provides a good natural drainage. The rotation field has, I think, the heaviest soil; that of the barley field is lighter. The Woburn soil is quite different; it is a deep soil consisting entirely of very fine sand. At the commencement of the experiments it was in a foul condition, a fact which disturbs the earliest results; it has since proved very fertile. It contains, however, but little lime.

1.—Residues of Nitrates.

The first point to which I would call attention is the difference in the behaviour of residues of ammonia salts and nitrates on these two soils. At Rothamsted, since 1852, there have been two plots (plots 17 and 18) in the wheat field on which the manures have alternated each year. Every spring[1] one plot receives as a top dressing 400 lbs. of ammonia salts

---

[1] The application has been in the spring since 1878.

per acre, while the next year the same plot receives no ammonia, but instead superphosphate with potash salts ; in the following year it has ammonia again. On the other plot the same treatment is pursued, but the applications of ammonia fall in alternate years with the applications to the first plot. By comparing the produce of these plots with that of a plot to which only superphosphate and potash salts are applied, we are able to ascertain what is the increase of crop yielded by the ammonia salts in the year of their application, and what after effect, if any, can be recognised in the second year, when no ammonia is applied. At Woburn a similar experiment is carried out both with wheat and barley, and the trial is extended so as to include nitrate of soda as well as ammonia salts. The ammonia salts at Rothamsted supply about 86 lbs. of nitrogen, and the ammonia salts and nitrate at Woburn about 82 lbs., per acre. In the following table the average results of eleven years, 1882–92, are given, as in this period we can compare all the results during the same seasons.

TABLE I.—INCREASE OF WHEAT AND BARLEY GIVEN BY AMMONIA SALTS AND NITRATE OF SODA IN THE FIRST YEAR, AND IN THE YEAR FOLLOWING THEIR APPLICATION. AVERAGE RESULTS OF ELEVEN YEARS, 1882–92.

	Rothamsted	Woburn			
	Wheat	Wheat		Barley	
	Ammonia Salts	Nitrate of Soda	Ammonia Salts	Nitrate of Soda	Ammonia Salts
First Year . .	Bushels 19·0	Bushels 21·2	Bushels 24·1	Bushels 30·7	Bushels 27·6
Second Year .	·1	·4	5·2	8·0	10·1
Total .	19·1	21·6	29·3	38·7	37·7
First Year . .	Per cent. 99·4	Per cent. 98·1	Per cent. 82·2	Per cent. 79·3	Per cent. 73·2
Second Year .	·6	1·9	17·8	20·7	26·8
Total . .	100·0	100·0	100·0	100·0	100·0

At Rothamsted the ammonia salts applied to wheat produce no effect in the year following their application. At Woburn, when nitrate of soda is applied to wheat, there is almost an entire absence of effect in the second year. The remaining experiments at Woburn show a very different result. In some seasons the residues of the ammonia and nitrate produce no effect, while in other seasons their effect is very marked; indeed, when ammonia salts are applied to barley, fully one-quarter of the return from the manure falls, on an average, in the second year. It will be observed that in every case the subsequent effect is greater with the ammonia salts than with nitrate.

We have probably a key to the explanation of these results in the character of the Woburn soil. As this soil contains very little lime, the nitrification of the ammonia is probably delayed, especially if the season be dry, and is not completed till the crop has passed the stage in which it can make use of nitrates. In the Rothamsted field the unused nitrates would be partly removed by the drain-pipes during autumn or winter, or carried to a depth at which they could no longer benefit a crop. At Woburn there are no drain-pipes; the unused nitrates would thus, after harvest, retire into the subsoil, and may be brought again to approach the surface by a rise in the water-level, or possibly by capillary attraction. A rise of the water-level in the subsoil is known in India and California to bring about an accumulation of salts in the top soil. The physical condition of a very fine uniform sand is also far more favourable to considerable movements of soil solutions than is the case with a tenacious clay, and a much greater quantity of water will be raised by capillary action in such a soil, though not to quite so great a height as the much smaller quantity of water rising in a clay. The nitrate of soda, being at once ready for assimilation, is more completely taken up by the crop, and less remains for a second season; and this residue is far smaller with wheat than with barley, probably owing to the earlier and deeper development of the roots in the case of autumn-sown wheat. The return from residues of ammonia salts and nitrates observed at Woburn is probably exceptional, but the possibility of such a return should be borne in mind.

2.—*Effect of Residues on Sugar-Beet.*

The Rothamsted experiments furnish many striking instances of the substantial effects produced on subsequent crops by the residues of previous applications of manure. Let me call your attention to one instructive instance which was not mentioned by Messrs. Lawes and Gilbert in their recent paper. In the field devoted to roots, the same manures had been applied annually for eighteen years, the first fifteen years to swedes, and the last three years to sugar-beet. Then came an interval of two years in which no nitrogenous manures were applied, but during which sugar-beet was grown as before. In the table opposite we have the average produce of the sugar-beet during three years with manure, and in the second year after the manuring had ceased.

While the manures were applied each year, both nitrate of soda and rape cake gave a somewhat larger produce than farmyard manure; but when the manures ceased to be applied, the plot which had received farmyard manure gave by far the largest produce—indeed, the crop obtained from the residue of this manure was practically equal to that previously obtained when the manure was annually applied.

The yield of the plots which had received the other nitrogenous manures is very instructive; there is in all cases a considerable excess of produce due to the previous manuring. This excess is much the greatest where rape cake had been applied. The organic matter of which this manure is composed decomposes rather slowly in the soil, and there is thus a residue left after the first season to benefit future crops. The results also show a very distinct effect produced by the previous applications of ammonia salts and nitrate of soda; and, in the case of the latter, the excess of crop due to its action amounts to over 4 tons per acre. To what are we to attribute this apparent effect of residues of ammonia salts and nitrate of soda? There can, I think, be little doubt that the subsequent effect of these salts is in this case due to the ploughing in of the leaves of the sugar-beet during the three preceding years: the roots were in all cases carted off the land. The table shows that over 6 tons of leaves had thus been returned to the soil each year on the nitrate of soda

TABLE II.—INFLUENCE OF RESIDUES OF MANURE ON SUGAR-BEET, ROTHAMSTED.

Manures applied eighteen years, 1856-72. Per acre.	Average produce three years, 1871-73, with manure			Produce in second year, 1875, without manure			Increase over unmanured in 1875
	Roots	Leaves	Total	Roots	Leaves	Total	Total
	Ton Cwt.	Ton Cwt.	Ton Cwt.	Ton Cwt.	Ton Cwt.	Ton Cwt.	Ton Cwt.
No manure	6 ... 16	1 ...15	8 ...11	5 ... 9	1 ... 1	6 ... 10	—
Ammonia salts, 400 lbs.	13 ... 4	4 ... 8	17 ... 12	8 ... 0	1 ... 3	9 ... 3	2 ... 13
Nitrate of soda, 550 lbs.	19 ... 15	6 ... 3	25 ... 19	9 ... 5	1 ...12	10 ... 17	4 ... 7
Rape cake, 2,000 lbs.	17 ... 4	4 ... 1	21 ... 5	11 ... 17	1 ...10	13 ... 7	6 ... 17
Farmyard manure, 14 tons	16 ... 6	4 ... 6	20 ... 12	17 ... 5	2 ...11	19 ... 16	13 ... 6

plot, an amount which would probably be equivalent to an autumn dressing of 3 to 4 tons of farmyard manure. The manuring effect of these leaves on the subsequent crops furnishes us with a capital example of the conditions in which compensation may fairly be claimed for the use of nitrate of soda.

3.—Residues of Farmyard Manure.

We turn next to a series of results showing the return obtained from residues of farmyard manure. The barley field at Rothamsted supplies the most striking example of the long continued effect of farmyard manure. One plot received each year, for twenty years, 1852–71, 14 tons of farmyard manure; half of this plot has since been left unmanured. By the side of this is another plot which has been unmanured from the beginning of the experiment in 1852. If we stand between these plots in summer time every eye can see that the old farm-yard manure plot is still giving by much the larger produce. Thus in 1896 the old farmyard manure plot produced 22½ bushels of barley, while the unmanured plot at its side pro-duced 12⅝ bushels; the residue of the farmyard manure was thus yielding an excess of 10 bushels of barley twenty-five years after the farmyard manure had ceased to be applied.

The practical results of such an experiment are apt to be misunderstood. Can a tenant, on the basis of these results, claim to be compensated for farmyard manure applied twenty-years ago? He certainly might if his lease allowed him to crop his land continuously with barley for forty-five years in succession, and to sell the whole of the produce without making any return to the land. If he held his land under such conditions, the application of farmyard manure, even twenty-five years ago, might, on the evidence before us, con-stitute a substantial improvement, for which payment might be claimed. I need hardly say, however, that our farmers do not hold land on the terms we have mentioned.

In preparing for this lecture, I have asked myself, Is it not possible from the complete records of the Rothamsted experiments to calculate what would have been the value to an incoming tenant of the residues of farmyard manure occurring both in the barley field, and in the permanent grass experiments ? The question clearly admits of an answer, as we know exactly what crops the incoming tenant would have obtained from the residues of manure remaining in the land. In order to deal with this question in a practical manner, I have sought to ascertain, in the first place, what was the natural produce of the land before the farmyard manure was applied ; I have taken this as representing the fertility of the land when it was entered upon by the improving tenant. The improving tenant applies farmyard manure every year for a number of years, and then leaves the farm. He is followed by one who employs no manure on the land in question. What is the money value to him of the unexhausted improvements of his predecessor ? It appears to me that the second tenant is deriving substantial benefit so long as the produce of the land remains above what it was before the farmyard manure was applied, and that as soon as the crop falls to what it originally was without farmyard manure all practical benefit has ceased. The money value to the second tenant of the previous manuring is shown by the value of the excess of crop which this manuring produces, this excess being reckoned by subtracting from each crop the produce obtained before the application of manure commenced.

The produce of the unmanured plot 6^1, in the first year of the experiment, 1852, was 29 bushels of barley and $17\frac{1}{2}$ cwts. of straw ; in the first five years of the experiment the average produce of the same plot was $28\frac{1}{2}$ bushels, and $16\frac{3}{4}$ cwts. of straw. As it is impossible to say that the first season was one of average produce, I adopt the mean of the first five years as indicating the producing power of the soil when the first tenant commenced his operations. In adopting this mean of five years we have more probably put the original fertility of the soil too low than too high. During twenty years, 1852–71, plot 7^1 received annually 14 tons of farmyard manure, ploughed in in spring before sowing the barley ; the average produce during this period was $48\frac{1}{4}$ bushels of barley, and $28\frac{1}{4}$ cwts. of straw.

We assume that the second tenant now enters on the land, and leaves the field unmanured. The average produce of barley during the first five years without manure was $39\frac{1}{4}$ bushels; in the second five years, $29\frac{1}{4}$ bushels; in the third five years, $30\frac{2}{3}$ bushels; in the fourth five years $22\frac{1}{2}$ bushels; in the fifth five years, 24 bushels. It is quite clear that during the last ten years the land has been yielding less than it did before any farmyard manure had been applied, and that there was then no residue of manure remaining on which compensation could fairly be claimed. On looking into the details of the third five years, we see that the produce in the last two years of the period was below $28\frac{1}{2}$ bushels. We have therefore thirteen years as the period during which the second tenant derived a substantial benefit from the previous applications of farmyard manure. During these thirteen years, 1872–84, the land (plot 7^1) has produced $441\frac{2}{3}$ bushels of barley, and $237\frac{1}{4}$ cwts. of straw. At its original rate of produce, before any farmyard manure was applied, it should have yielded $370\frac{1}{2}$ bushels, and $217\frac{3}{4}$ cwts. of straw. The advantage to the second tenant of the manure applied by his predecessor is thus represented by $71\frac{1}{8}$ bushels of barley, and $19\frac{3}{8}$ cwts. of barley straw. If we reckon the barley as worth $3s.$ a bushel, we have £10. $13s.$ as the gross return per acre received by the second tenant in consequence of the previous application of 14 tons of dung every year for twenty years. From this gross return we have to deduct the expenses of harvesting and marketing 71 bushels; we have also to bear in mind that the return in crop is spread over thirteen years, and that the compensation to be paid to the first tenant really therefore represents a capital sum spent in the purchase of an annuity. These circumstances alone considerably reduce the sum to be paid by the second tenant on entering the farm, without taking into account any margin to cover risk, or any profit on the transaction which he may fairly expect to make.

The experiment we have quoted only allows us to value the unexhausted residue of the dung in terms of the barley it was capable of producing; had the second tenant grown other crops, as mangel and clover, the money value of the residue would have appeared much more considerable.

Our next illustration is from the permanent grass experiments at Rothamsted. In Rothamsted Park, plot 2 received annually for eight years, 1856-63, 14 tons of farmyard manure, and has since been left unmanured. Calculating precisely as before the practical value of the residue of this manure, it appears that for nine years it yielded a produce greater than that given by the land before farmyard manure was applied; and that during these nine years it produced a total excess of crop amounting to 6 tons of hay per acre. Valuing hay at 70s. a ton, we obtain £21 as the gross return per acre from the residue of the farmyard manure. From this gross sum serious deductions have to be made on the lines already mentioned, if we would arrive at the sum fairly due to an outgoing tenant as compensation for the unexhausted value of his manure.

The far greater compensation due in the case of the grass land, notwithstanding the much smaller manure residue involved, teaches us an important lesson. It will always be the case that slowly acting manures, if really suitable to the soil, will yield a larger return on grass than on arable land. On permanent grass land any waste of plant food in the soil is reduced to a minimum.

At Woburn, in the experiments conducted by the Royal Agricultural Society on the continuous growth of wheat and barley, there are plots on which well-rotted farmyard manure has been applied as a top-dressing during twenty years, 1877-96. After the first five years the plots were in each case divided, one-half being subsequently unmanured, while on the other half the farmyard manure was continuously applied. We have thus, both in the barley and wheat field, plots which received farmyard manure for five years, and have for fifteen years been cropped without manure. Such an experiment should supply us with facts very pertinent to the question before us; the results obtained are, however, somewhat difficult to interpret.

The manure used in these experiments was prepared by feeding fattening bullocks in deep stalls having concrete sides and bottom. These bullocks received decorticated cotton-cake, maize meal, turnips, and straw chaff. The whole of the food and litter employed was weighed, and its composition ascertained by chemical analysis; it was thus known how

B

much nitrogen as food and litter had been employed in the preparation of one ton of manure. The manure was not removed from under the animal till the whole of the desired quantity had been produced; it was then clamped, and finally applied to the land as a top-dressing in a well-rotted condition. On the wheat land the manure was applied towards the end of January; on the barley land, as soon as the plant was up. The dressing of manure on plot 11, the experiment we are about to discuss, would weigh about 7 tons per acre, and is estimated to contain 164 lbs. of nitrogen, equal to 200 lbs. of ammonia.[1]

In the barley field, the average produce during the five years while the manure was applied—1877–81—amounted to 35·7 bushels. In the first five years after the manure ceased, the average produce was 37·7 bushels; in the second five years, 31·3 bushels; in the third five years, 28·1 bushels. The inferior produce of the five years with manure is due to the foul condition of the land at the commencement of the experiment, and to the bad seasons.

The two facts just mentioned occasion much difficulty in deciding what was the original capacity of the land for producing barley. The average produce of the two unmanured plots in the first season (1877) was 21·1 bushels, and in the first five seasons 23·8 bushels. The average produce of the same plots in the first ten seasons is, however, 25 bushels of corn, and 14⅝ cwts. of straw. As we must suppose that the fertility of the land was greater at the commencement of the experiment than is shown by an average of ten years without manure, it seems safer to take 26 bushels of corn, and 15 cwts. of straw, as our estimate of the producing capacity of the land for barley at the commencement of the experiment.

The figures already quoted show that the average produce of the land had not fallen below 26 bushels during the fifteen years after the manure had ceased to be applied, though it seems to have nearly reached that point. The total produce

---

[1] The manure in question was made from food and litter, containing 188 lbs. of nitrogen. The quantity of nitrogen in the manure is not known. The estimate adopted by the experimenters is calculated from the ratio between food and manure employed by Lawes and Gilbert many years ago, and in which the losses occurring in the dung-heap are not taken into account.

of barley on this plot during the fifteen years 1882–96 was 485 bushels of corn, and 272 cwts. of straw; from this we have to deduct 390 bushels of corn, and 225 cwts. of straw, as representing the producing power of the original soil. We have thus 95 bushels of corn, and 47 cwts. of straw, as apparently due to the residue of manure remaining in the soil after five small dressings of rich manure. The quantity of manure contributing to the residue was, however, in fact somewhat larger, as, owing to a mistake, the farmyard manure was in one year (1888) put on plot 11a, which should have had none, instead of on plot 11b, which was intended to be continuously manured. The error has been partly corrected by summing in each case only the manured or unmanured produce; but the error due to the introduction of a new residue of manure still remains. Reckoning the 95 bushels of barley at 3s. a bushel, its value will be £14. 5s. 0d.

We turn now to the corresponding experiment with wheat. We have here 22·9 bushels as the average produce of five years with farmyard manure, and 20·7, 20·1, and 16·3 bushels as the average produce of the first, second, and third five years without manure. In the case of the wheat we are, if possible, in a greater difficulty as to the producing capacity of the land at the beginning of the experiment. The mean produce of the two unmanured plots in the first year was 21·5 bushels; in the first five years, 16¼ bushels; and in the first ten years 17·2 bushels of corn, and 17⅜ cwts. of straw. Adopting, as before, the latter figure as the nearest approximation to the truth, we take 18 bushels as representing the original wheat-producing capacity of the land, with 17½ cwts. of straw.

The average produce of plot 11a keeps above the estimated original producing capacity of the land for thirteen years (1882–94), during which time the total produce has amounted to 259·6 bushels of corn, and 234¼ cwts. of straw. Deducting the 234 bushels and 227½ cwts. corresponding to the original productive capacity of the land, we have in round numbers 26 bushels of wheat, and 7 cwts. of straw, as representing the effect of the residue of manure. The wheat at 4s. a bushel will be worth £5. 4s.

Thus, both in the experiments on the heavy land at Rothamsted, and on the sandy soil at Woburn, it has appeared that the effect of long continued previous applications of dung is exhausted on land cultivated for barley or wheat in thirteen or fifteen years. We may arrive at the same conclusion by looking at another feature of these experiments.

If a dressing of manure, continuously applied during many years, is not excessive in quantity—that is, if the manuring power of the dressing and of its residues is insufficient to produce the highest crops which the soil could yield in an average season—the produce of the land will be found to increase year by year till the time is reached when the earliest dressings of the manure cease to affect the crop; after this stage has been gained the annual produce will remain unaltered, save by variations in the character of the seasons, the influences of past residues having now become a constant quantity. The following table shows the average produce of wheat and barley at Rothamsted in successive periods of five and ten years, the land receiving every year 14 tons of ordinary yard manure per acre. The produce of wheat and barley in successive periods at Woburn, the land receiving annually 7 to 8 tons of cake-fed manure, is also given :—

TABLE III.—PRODUCE OF WHEAT AND BARLEY AT ROTHAMSTED CONTINUOUSLY MANURED WITH FARMYARD MANURE.

Wheat : Broadbalk Field, Plot 2			Barley : Hoos Field, Plot 7		
Ten years' average	Five years' average	Periods	Ten years' average	Five years' average	Periods
Bushels	Bushels		Bushels	Bushels	
27·0	27·0	1844–48	45·0	41·5	1852–56
	27·1	1849.53		48.5	1857–61
37·8	38·4	1854–58	51·5	55·4	1862.66
	37·1	1859–63		47·6	1867–71
35·3	35·8	1864–68	50·3	49·6	1872–76
	34·8	1869–73		50·8	1877.81
29·8	28·9	1874–78	47·6	53·4	1882–86
	30·5	1879–83		41·9	1887 91
38·9	36·4	1884–88	—	50·3	1892–96
	41·4	1889–93			

SIMILAR EXPERIMENTS AT WOBURN.

Wheat : Stackyard Field, Plot 11b			Barley : Stackyard Field, Plot 11b		
Ten years' average	Five years' average	Periods	Ten years' average	Five years' average	Periods
Bushels	Bushels		Bushels	Bushels	
26·8	22·9	1877–81	40·1	35·8	1877–81
	30·6	1882–86		44·4	1882–86
27·8	31·8	1887–91	39·6	87·9	1887–91
	23·9	1892–96		41·3	1892–96

We see that at Rothamsted both the wheat and barley crops reached their maximum in the third period of five years from the commencement of the annual applications of manure. At Woburn the same result appears in the wheat experiment, but with the barley the maximum crop is reached in the second five years. These results are in general agreement with the conclusions we have already come to from a study of the crops yielded by land on which the applications of manure had ceased. It will be remarked that in every case the barley responds more quickly to the manure than wheat. The cultivation of the soil in spring time, which is a necessary accompaniment of sowing barley, is indeed highly favourable to the nitrification of residues of organic manure and to their utilisation by the crop.

I have already incidentally reminded you that residues of farmyard manure in the soil will produce no visible effect on subsequent crops if these are too liberally manured. If an incoming tenant, after paying for the residues of manure left by his predecessor, proceeds to treat his land with dressings of manure sufficient to yield the heaviest crops which the soil and season admit of, he will derive no benefit from the previous residues. Nor must we suppose that, if the crops are not then benefited, the residues of previous manures will necessarily remain in the soil for future use. This is indeed partially true if the residues consist of phosphates or potash ; but it is not true when the residue consists of nitrogenous organic matter, as this will be wasted by the process of nitrification in the soil, even if the nitrates thus formed are not taken up by a crop. To obtain the greatest return from manure, or from its residues, it is necessary that the crops produced should be distinctly below the highest which the soil and season would produce with an abundant manuring. It is only when manure is very cheap, or crops are fetching a high price, that high farming will be true economy.

Even when the quantity of manure applied to the land is insufficient to entirely obliterate the visible effect of the residues of previous manuring, the return in the crop obtained from these residues may be considerably diminished in consequence of this subsequent manuring; and this will be especially the case when we have to do with a residue of farmyard, or other nitrogenous manure, and are growing not corn but green crops. To make myself clear I must remind you that green crops, as turnips or grass, may vary very much in composition. As an illustration let me take the swedes grown in the experimental rotation field at Rothamsted. On one portion of this field the swedes have been grown for many years with superphosphate only. On another portion of the field a liberal nitrogenous manuring is applied with the superphosphate. In 1880 the superphosphate gave nearly 12 tons of swedes, and the mixed manure 22 tons. Analysis showed that 1 ton of swedes grown with nitrogenous manure contained one-half more nitrogen than 1 ton of swedes grown with superphosphate; the same quantity of soil nitrogen which would produce 3 tons of swedes with superphosphate alone would thus only yield 2 tons when high manuring was adopted. Thus under a generous treatment of the land, and especially with the growth of green crops, the apparent effect of residues of nitrogenous manure will be considerably diminished, and their effect will appear partly in an alteration in the composition of the subsequent crops instead of in an increase in their weight.

It is evident from what has now been said that under the conditions of ordinary agriculture we must not expect to obtain the large returns from residues of farmyard manure which were obtained at Rothamsted and Woburn by leaving the land for many years without manure. The treatment of the land which resulted in this large return from previous residues was however attended with an entire loss of its previous high condition, and reduced the soil to a low state of fertility, a result which cannot generally be desirable.

4.—*Rotation Experiments at Rothamsted.*

We turn now from the simple conditions attending the continuous cultivation of grass, or of wheat, or barley, to the much more complicated conditions which are met with in a rotation. Fortunately for our purpose experimental rotations have been carried on for many years, both at Rothamsted and at Woburn, under various systems of manuring.

The rotation experiments at Rothamsted commenced in 1848, and have been carried on now for fifty years on one uniform plan.[1] The field is divided into three equal parts, on one of which no manure has been applied from the commencement. On another, the swedes are grown with mineral superphosphate only, to which in the last three rotations salts supplying potash, soda, and magnesia have been added. On a third division the swedes have always received the superphosphate and the salts just named, and in addition a liberal nitrogenous manuring, consisting of 2,000 lbs. of powdered rape-cake, and 200 lbs. of ammonium salts, supplying in all about 141 lbs. of nitrogen per acre. No other crop besides the swedes has ever been manured.

The rotation followed is the ordinary four-course, consisting of swedes, barley, clover or beans, and wheat. On one half of each division the turnips have been fed off by sheep, or in later years sliced and ploughed in ; on the other half, the whole of the turnip crop is carted off the field. In the third year of each rotation one half of each division is treated as a bare fallow, the other half being in clover or beans. There are thus four plots in each division:— (1) Turnips fed, third year clover ; (2) turnips fed, third year fallow ; (3) turnips carted, third year clover ; (4) turnips carted, third year fallow.

[1] Details of these experiments will be found in the *Journ. of the Roy. Agri. Society,* 1894, 585.

Before entering upon the main teaching of this rotation, I would call your attention to one very curious result, namely, the action of residues of superphosphate upon the clover crop. I have already mentioned that one division of the field has been cultivated without the use of any manure, while the middle division, during the first nine rotations, received $3\frac{1}{2}$ cwts. of mineral superphosphate with the turnips. The power of producing clover was originally equal on both divisions, for the first clover crop in 1850 amounted to 6,200 lbs. of hay per acre on the unmanured portion, and to 6,362 lbs. where the turnips had received superphosphate. The subsequent clover crops are, however, very different in the two divisions, the land receiving superphosphate yielding generally two or three times as much clover as the land entirely unmanured. The crops of clover-hay per acre were as follows :—

—	Unmanured	Superphosphate for swedes
	lbs.	lbs.
1874	2,668	5,640
1882	2,714	7,314
1886	1,295	4,810
1894	1,841	6,678
Mean . .	2,129	6,110

In the last two years mentioned above the swedes received potash salts as well as superphosphate, but it is evident that the difference we refer to occurred when only superphosphate was applied.

This great effect, produced by the residue from a moderate application of superphosphate, is probably due to a considerable extent to the gypsum which the superphosphate supplied. The sulphuric acid of the gypsum is very probably the active constituent. We sometimes forget in our manuring experiments, that albuminoids, in which the clover crop is so rich, cannot be produced without sulphur.

It is clear that in the experiment just quoted the money value of the residue of the superphosphate far exceeded the original cost of the manure. It is equally clear, I think, to all of us, that no such value can be attached to the ordinary use of superphosphate. Where a neglected soil is being brought into good condition, the effect of superphosphate and of its residue in the soil may be very great; but superphosphate and other sulphates are so largely used in ordinary agriculture, and the soil is generally so well supplied with their residues, that the application or omission of a dressing in the last rotation of an outgoing tenant can make scarcely any difference to his successor.

We will now inquire what the rotation experiments have to teach us as to the effect which carting off the swedes has upon the subsequent crop of the rotation. Omitting the first rotation, which served to equalise the land, and three other rotations in which the turnip crop failed, or was very small, there remain eight rotations suitable for our present inquiry.

Where the swedes had received the ample nitrogenous manuring, the average produce in these eight rotations was 19 tons $6\frac{1}{4}$ cwts. of roots on the two plots from which the roots were carted. The removal of these roots with their leaves caused the succeeding crop of barley to be on an average $9\frac{3}{4}$ bushels less than on the corresponding two plots on which the swedes were fed, or cut up and ploughed into the soil. In round numbers we may say that on this highly manured land the removal of 10 tons of swedes with their leaves diminished the following crop of barley by 5 bushels.

Where the rotation has received no nitrogenous manure for fifty years, the swedes being grown with superphosphate, and latterly with superphosphate and potash salts, the average crop of roots carted in the eight rotations has been 9 tons $8\frac{1}{2}$ cwts. The carting of these roots, with their leaves, has on an average diminished the succeeding crop of barley by $8\frac{3}{4}$ bushels; or, in round numbers, the removal of 10 tons of roots has occasioned a loss of 9 bushels of barley.

It is obvious that the barley crop has been much more affected by the removal of the roots on the poorer than on the richer land. The average loss of barley on the highly manured plots is, however, possibly too low, as in two years (1858 and 1889) out of the eight the removal of the roots did not sensibly affect the succeeding barley crops on these plots, while the removal of the roots was always felt on the superphosphate plots. On the other hand, we have to remark that the great apparent loss of barley on the superphosphate plots is confined to the three years when the roots not carted were fed off on the land by sheep; in the five years in which the turnips were sliced and ploughed in, the carting of 9 tons $4\frac{1}{4}$ cwts. of roots occasioned an average loss of $5\frac{6}{8}$ bushels of barley, a rate not very different from that shown on the highly manured division. It seems possible that the sheep feeding off the turnips grown by superphosphate alone, without any cake or corn in addition, and with a minimum of straw chaff, were in a condition of nitrogen starvation, and that more nitrogen passed in their urine to the soil than was supplied by their food.[1] It was known, indeed, as a fact, that the sheep rapidly fell off in condition. In consequence of this manuring of the land by the sheep, the plots where the turnips were fed off would yield more barley than they should have done, and the injurious effect of carting the turnips on the other plots was thus exaggerated. Looking at the whole of the results, we shall perhaps be near the truth if we assume that the carting of 10 tons of swedes with their leaves may be expected usually to diminish the following barley crop by about 6 bushels.

What has been the effect of carting the turnip crop upon the other crops of the rotation? To answer this question we will take the mean of ten rotations, including all except the first, and the one in which the turnip crop entirely failed. Looking first at the richer land, where the swedes received an abundance of nitrogenous manure, we find that the entire removal of the roots, averaging 16 tons $15\frac{6}{8}$ cwts. in each rotation, produced practically no effect upon the other crops in the rotation, with the exception of the barley already noticed. The exhaustion produced by carting is not shown in the turnip crop, for this is on an average half a ton better on the plots where the turnips had been carted. It is perceived

---

[1] If the swedes contained ·4 per cent. of true albuminoids (·394 per cent. was found by analysis in the superphosphate swedes of 1880), the sheep would daily have to consume turnips equal to one-quarter of their live weight to preserve a condition of nitrogen equilibrium.

but little in the bean and clover crops,[1] as their annual produce is only reduced by 382 lbs. per acre where the turnips have been carted. It is finally not shown by the wheat, the wheat crops yielded by the plots where the roots were carted being practically identical with those yielded where the roots were fed.

If we turn now to the division of the field receiving superphosphate, but no nitrogenous manure, we find not only the greater diminution of the barley crop following the carting of the roots, which we have already noticed, but we find that the other crops in the rotation are also diminished to a small but sensible extent. The carting, on an average, of 8 tons of swedes, with their leaves, in each rotation, has apparently diminished the swede crop on these plots by 1 ton 7 cwts. of roots; has diminished the bean and clover crops by 563 lbs.; and has decreased the wheat crop by 2½ bushels per acre. The carting of 8 tons of swedes in this exhausted division of the field has thus been attended with worse results than the carting of 16 tons on the more liberally treated plots. We have before had examples of the considerable results produced on poor land by small residues of manure; we now see another side of the same fact, namely, the sensitiveness of poor land to any process of exhaustion.

We will now go a step further, and inquire what has been the return in the various crops of the rotation for the large amount of nitrogenous manure, equivalent to about 1 to 1½ ton of cake per acre, applied to the swede crop in the upper division of the field. In dealing with this question we will take the average crops of eleven rotations, as in all of these the nitrogenous manure was applied, although in one rotation no roots were grown. The average results of these eleven rotations will be found in Table IV.

In order to estimate the practical effect of the nitrogenous manure, we require to know what would have been the produce of the land without its application; to ascertain this starting-point correctly is a difficulty which attends all trials

[1] In order to obtain one figure representing the leguminous crops in the rotation, the total weight of the bean crops, corn and straw, and of the clover crops weighed as hay, are summed together, and given as tons or pounds per acre.

of manures. The usual plan of deducting the produce of a similar piece of land, to which the manure under examination has not been applied, is generally the only course open to us. This method, however, leads not unfrequently to serious error when we take the produce of a *continuously unmanured* plot as the basis for our calculation. The produce of such a plot is certain to diminish seriously as time goes on, and if we deduct the produce of this exhausted land from the produce obtained by manuring, we are virtually putting to the credit of the manure the fertility lost on the unmanured plot.[1] Bearing these considerations in mind, we take the mean produce of the two plots on which the roots were fed or ploughed in, in the superphosphate division of the field, as representing most nearly the original productiveness of the land without nitrogenous manure. Subtracting the mean produce of these plots from the mean produce of the two corresponding plots in the division receiving nitrogenous manure, we find, as the result of that manuring, the production of 7 tons of roots consumed by sheep, and the subsequent production of $10\frac{1}{4}$ bushels of barley and $\frac{1}{4}$ bushel of wheat, with, on the bean and clover plot, 845 lbs. of mixed clover hay, and bean crop. If we take the four clover crops only, which, however, fell in the later years of the experiment, 1874, 1882, 1886, 1894, we have an average produce on the superphosphate plot of 2 tons 18 cwts., and on the plot having nitrogenous manure of 3 tons 7 cwts. of hay; the mean excess of clover-hay on the plot receiving nitrogenous manure was thus 9 cwts. In the seven bean crops, the mean produce on the superphosphate plot was $16\frac{1}{4}$ bushels, and on the plot receiving nitrogenous manure $23\frac{3}{4}$ bushels; there was a difference therefore in favour of the latter of $7\frac{1}{4}$ bushels.

We have here the result of the most exhaustive trial which has yet been made of the influence of nitrogenous manure in a rotation. From our present point of view we may consider the manure to have been applied to the turnips by the outgoing tenant; he feeds the roots on the land, and claims

[1] The only truly accurate method of ascertaining the comparative value of different manures is to experiment at the same time with various quantities of each. Those quantities of manure which yield *the same amount of produce* are clearly those which have an equivalent value.

Table IV.—Agdell Rotation Field, Rothamsted.

Mean produce per Acre of Eleven Rotations, 1852–95.

—	Unmanured				Superphosphate, 3½ cwts. per acre (last three rotations with potash, soda, and magnesia added)				Nitrogenous manure; 141 lbs. nitrogen per acre, with superphosphate, potash, soda, and magnesia			
	Roots carted		Roots fed		Roots carted		Roots fed		Roots carted		Roots fed	
	Fallow	Beans or clover	Fallow	Beans or clover[2]	Fallow	Beans or clover	Fallow	Beans or clover	Fallow	Beans or clover	Fallow	Beans or clover
Swedes[1] (tons and cwts.) . .	1 5⅛	0 14¾	1 4¾	0 14¾	8 0⅛	7 19¾	9 0⅜	9 13⅜	16 15⅛	16 16⅛	16 17⅛	15 13½
Barley (bushels) . . .	26⅜	27⅛	27¼	24¼	23⅝	25⅛	30⅝	35⅛	34⅞	38¼	42⅝	43½
Beans or Clover (lbs.) . .	—	1,917	—	1,840	—	3,477	—	3,997	—	4,488	—	4,842
Wheat (bushels) . . .	28¾	26	28¼	23⅞	32	31¾	33¼	35	33¼	35⅛	33	35⅝

[1] Average of ten rotations.

[2] The produce on this plot is apparently reduced by a depression in the land.

from the next tenant the unexhausted value of his manuring. He has applied 141 lbs. of nitrogen per acre, chiefly in the form of oil-cake. This quantity of nitrogen would be contained in about 18 cwts. of decorticated cotton-cake, costing at wholesale price £5; or in 22 to 30 cwts. of linseed-cake (according to composition), costing from £8 to £12. The cake is employed in this experiment as a manure, and not as a food; its effect on the following crops is thus the maximum effect it is capable of producing. In only five of the eleven rotations were the turnips actually fed by sheep on the land; in five the whole crop of turnips was sliced and ploughed in; and in one rotation the turnips failed, and the manure which had been applied was left in the land for the succeeding crops. Had the cake been given as food to sheep consuming the turnips, a notable proportion of the nitrogen would have been lost to the land. Had the cake been fed to bullocks at the farm buildings, and the manure from the bullocks applied to the turnips, a much larger proportion of the nitrogen would have been lost, and the remainder left in a more inert condition. We have here then a maximum result, from which large deductions must be made before it can be considered applicable to the conditions of our ordinary agriculture.

The valuation of the crops yielded by the residue of the nitrogenous manure gives the following result:—The $10\frac{1}{4}$ bushels of barley and $\frac{1}{4}$ bushel of wheat will be worth, at our previous estimates, £1. 11s. 9d.; to this we may add either $7\frac{1}{4}$ bushels of beans, worth £1. 9s., or 9 cwts. of clover-hay, worth £2. The total valuation is thus £3. 6s. 3d., if we assume that the two leguminous crops will alternate in a series of rotations; there will be also in addition a little barley and bean straw. If we assume that the nitrogenous manure was applied in the form of decorticated cotton-cake, at the cost of £5, we have (besides the feeding value of 7 tons of swedes) a gross return in subsequent crops representing 66 per cent. of the cost of the cake. If instead of cotton-cake linseed-cake had been employed, the return in the subsequent crops would represent about 33 per cent. of the cost of the cake. From this gross return the second tenant has of course to deduct the expenses he must go through to realise these crops, the cost of cultivation, harvesting, and marketing. In estimating the sum he can afford to pay for the residue of manure left by his predecessor, he will also recollect that he will not himself be repaid in crops for two years after his entrance on the farm.

There is clear evidence that the effect of the liberal quantity of cake applied in these experiments was confined to the first three crops (two years) after its application ; the wheat, which comes at the end of the rotation, shows no benefit from the cake applied to the turnips ; and this is equally the case whether the wheat is preceded by a leguminous crop or by a bare fallow.

5.—Rotation Experiments at Woburn.

In the rotation experiments at Woburn an attempt has been made to determine the comparative effect of two manures prepared respectively by the consumption of equal weights of decorticated cotton-cake and maize-meal, and which ought therefore to contain very different quantities of nitrogen. The investigation has been continued during twenty years : it can hardly be said to have attained its object, but the results are nevertheless extremely instructive.[1]

The rotation experiments at Woburn commenced in 1877. They were so arranged that four rotations in different stages proceeded simultaneously ; each crop in the rotation was thus grown every year.

During the first eight years the roots were manured with dung made by feeding bullocks in deep stalls or boxes, one set of bullocks receiving 1,000 lbs. of decorticated cotton-cake, and the other set 1,000 lbs. of maize-meal; the turnips, chaff, and litter supplied being in both cases the same quantity. The cake employed would contain about 50 lbs. more nitrogen than the maize, but the actual difference in the resulting manures was not ascertained. In eight crops of roots thus manured in successive years, the excess yielded by the cake over the maize manure averaged only $12\frac{3}{4}$ cwts. per acre. The roots were fed off by sheep, and the crop of barley

---

[1] A detailed report on these experiments has been published by Dr. J. A. Voelcker, *Journ. Roy. Agri. Society*, 1897, 622.

following showed only $\frac{1}{2}$ bushel to the credit of the cake manure. The succeeding clover was fed off on the land by sheep; on the cake plot the sheep received 728 lbs. of decorticated cotton-cake, and on the maize plot 728 lbs. of maize-meal. The wheat following the clover showed, on an average, about 1 bushel of wheat in favour of the maize plot. The richer manure thus gave, on the whole, no greater crops than the poorer.

The absence of any practical result from the excess of nitrogen, known to have been applied on the cake plots, was probably due to the presence in the soils of *all* the plots of a supply of available nitrogen quite sufficient for the production of crops as large as the other conditions of soil and season would admit of. The swedes, in fact, averaged 17 tons, the barley 46 bushels, and the wheat $41\frac{1}{2}$ bushels per acre, a produce very good for the light land in question.[1]

It is important to remember that the utilisation of nitrogenous organic manures by crops is sharply limited by several conditions. The amount of nitrogen in the soil has no influence on its fertility, except so far as it leads to the production of nitrates; the limitations to nitrification may thus constitute an obstacle preventing the growth of bigger crops. Imperfections in tillage, a deficiency or excess of water in the soil, the presence of an excess of readily oxidisable organic matter, or a lack of carbonate of lime, may each of them effectually limit the fertility of the land, notwithstanding the application of large quantities of farmyard manure.

If the limitation is not due to an inadequate production of nitrates in the soil, it may be due to an inadequate supply of some of the ash constituents required by crops. The more

---

[1] Dr. Voelcker's remarks on this point may be quoted:—" On comparing the produce of the wheat and barley on these rotation plots with that obtained on the adjoining permanent corn plots, highly manured every year, it was found that the average produce of wheat on the maize-meal plot was higher than the highest average produce, viz. 38·8 bushels, obtained during the corresponding years on the permanent wheat plots; and that the average produce of the barley was also nearly as high as that of the most highly manured plots of the permanent barley. From this it appeared that, even with the poorer maize-meal manuring, crops of wheat and barley about as heavy as the land could produce were actually obtained. This being so, it would not be possible for the richer cotton-cake to give more than the maximum yield for the land, and, accordingly, the difference between the richer and the poorer manuring could not be brought out."

rapid is the growth of a crop—and growth must be rapid if a large produce is to be obtained—the more liberal must be the supply in the soil of phosphates, alkalies, and lime. Had the turnips just referred to received superphosphate, we should have expected larger crops of roots, and probably the two kinds of dung would have shown more difference in their effect on this crop.

When everything has been done for the land, we have still the stern limitations imposed by the character of the season, and especially by the supply of sunshine and rain throughout the growing period. Any supply of plant food in excess of the capabilities of the season is thrown away, a fact to be continually borne in mind by those pursuing high farming.

After having applied the manures described during two rotations without establishing any difference in their effect, a change was made, and one-half of all the plots was cultivated as before, but without any manure; moreover, on this portion of the field the whole of the roots (mangels) and the whole of the clover was removed from the land. The object in view was to see if by exhausting the land the crops would exhibit any greater produce where the larger amount of nitrogenous manure had been applied. The excess of nitrogen was due to the consumption of about $1\frac{1}{2}$ ton of decorticated cotton-cake in one case, and of $1\frac{1}{2}$ ton of maize-meal in the other case, the difference between the quantities of nitrogen in these foods being about 170 lbs. per acre. The quantities mentioned were distributed over the eight preceding years, the last portion of the manure having been applied two or three years before the commencement of the new unmanured rotations.

The first crops taken under the new system showed perhaps a small excess on the cotton-cake plot. Where the new system began with mangels, the first crops showed on an average no excess on the cotton-cake plot; where barley was the first crop there was an excess of $1\frac{1}{2}$ bushel; where peas, the excess was $4\frac{1}{2}$ bushels; where wheat, $1\frac{3}{4}$ bushel. That these small differences were really due to a residue of the previous cake manure must, however, be doubtful, as when

C

we look at the whole produce of three complete rotations without manuré, we find in the total no excess of produce on the former cake plot. This is in spite of the distinctly exhausted condition reached by the land, which is specially shown by a great diminution in the barley crop. It would appear, therefore, that in this case a moderate amount of cake manure, applied during two rotations, produced no distinct effect on the crops two years after its application had ceased. This result is in agreement with the fact observed in the Rothamsted rotation, where the application of a liberal nitrogenous manuring to the turnips produced no effect on the wheat, even when no clover crop was introduced.

We turn now to the later results from the other half of the rotation field at Woburn. On this the swedes were now grown with superphosphate only. An equal weight of roots was also now carted from each plot, leaving about six or seven tons, which were fed off by sheep, consuming in one case 400 lbs. of decorticated cotton-cake, and in the other case 400 lbs. of maize-meal per acre. All the remaining crops of the rotation were unmanured, and were entirely removed from the land.

On two other plots of the rotation neither cake nor corn was fed with the turnips, but the barley crop was manured with nitrate of soda, the quantities applied containing respectively 10 per cent. less nitrogen than was contained in the cotton-cake, and 15 per cent. less nitrogen than was contained in the maize.[1] By this means a comparison was instituted between the effect of nitrogen applied as sheep manure, and the effect of nitrogen applied as nitrate of soda. To make the comparison more exact, the quantities of phosphates and potash contained in the cake and maize (less that reckoned as assimilated by the sheep) were applied with the nitrate of soda to the barley plots. The average results of three rotations manured in this manner are shown in the following Table :—

[1] For the purposes of the Woburn experiments, it was assumed at their commencement in 1877, that 10 per cent. of the nitrogen of cake, and 15 per cent. of the nitrogen of maize, turnips, hay, and straw, are retained by the animal consuming them, or at least do not appear in the manure. We have already stated that this estimate is no longer generally accepted.

TABLE V.—MANURED ROTATION, WOBURN. MEAN PRODUCE PER ACRE, 1885-96.

—	400 lbs. maize fed with roots	400 lbs. cotton-cake fed with roots	Nitrate soda (equal to maize manure) to barley	Nitrate soda (equal to cake manure) to barley
Swedes, 1885-96 (tons, cwts.)	10 ... 10	10 ... 9½	10 ... 0¾	10 ... 10½
Barley, 1886-96 (bushels) .	34·7	37·7	34·5	40·6
Clover-hay, 1889-95(tons,cwts.)	2 ... 9	2 ... 7¾	2 ... 10¾	2 ... 11¼
Wheat, 1886-96 (bushels) .	32·4	33·9	32·1	33·0

Before considering the excess of produce obtained from the higher manuring, we must first inquire what was the excess of manure in each case. The cotton-cake consumed by the sheep contained 21-22 lbs. more nitrogen than the maize-meal eaten on the comparative plot ; this quantity of nitrogen purchased as decorticated cotton-cake would cost about 15s. at wholesale prices. The manure left in the land after the consumption of the cake by sheep has produced a crop of barley 3 bushels greater than that yielded by the corresponding manure from maize. We have thus a gross return of 9s. as the residual effect of the 15s. worth of cake consumed by sheep immediately before the sowing of the barley. The manure was apparently without effect on the succeeding clover and wheat crops ; the clover is a little less on the cotton-cake plot and the wheat a little more, and the money value of these differences compensate each other. The gross return is thus 60 per cent. on the cost of the cotton-cake, a result almost identical with that obtained at Rothamsted.

The heavier dressing of nitrate of soda applied to the barley would contain about 20 lbs. more nitrogen than the lighter dressing ; these 20 lbs. of nitrogen purchased as nitrate would cost nearly 9s. The increase in the crop of barley by the use of this nitrate of soda is 6 bushels, representing a gross return of 18s. The advantage resulting from the manure is probably confined to the barley crop; the differences shown by the clover and wheat are very slight. The nitrate of soda was thus far more profitable than the cake manure. To obtain the whole return from the cake we must, however, take into account the increase in live weight of the sheep consuming it.

The teaching of these Woburn rotation experiments is of a very practical character. They proclaim the fact that on land in high condition—which merely implies that the quantity of *available* plant food is for the time ample in relation to the assimilating power of the crops—the use of cake-fed manure in a rotation may not only be without immediate effect upon the crops, but may also leave no valuable residue in the land. Some of the causes which limit the effects of excessive applications of manure have been already mentioned; but why, we may ask, should the residue of this cake manure produce no effect when the land was subsequently left unmanured ?

In looking at this question we have to bear in mind that, in the case before us, the actual weight of manure applied was probably nearly the same both in the case of the cake-fed and of the maize-fed manure. Had the experiment consisted in a comparison of the effect of 10 tons and 20 tons of farm-yard manure in a rotation, the more liberal manuring would pretty certainly have shown a distinct after effect when the land was cultivated without manure, for the larger quantity of manure would longer have resisted the oxidising processes always proceeding in the soil. The comparison is, however, between two equal quantities of dung, both of them small dressings, but one richer in soluble nitrogenous matter than the other. Both of these dressings would disappear from the soil by natural oxidation at the same time; and if the products of their oxidation produce no effect on the crops during the first two years, nothing is to be expected from them afterwards.

It is important always to remember that while the use of oil-cake to enrich manure may produce a marked effect on the crop to which the manure is immediately applied, it does not appreciably increase the length of time through which the effect of the manure will be perceived. The difference between the first effect and the after effect will be greater with rich manure than with poor. The characteristic of cake-fed manure is that a larger proportion of its nitrogen is immediately available as plant food. The after effects of rich and poor manure will be far more alike than their first effect.

The rapidity with which applications of organic manure will disappear in the soil depends upon their quantity, and on the rapidity of the oxidation proceeding in the soil, the manure disappearing much more rapidly in some soils than in others. In all the instances we have quoted in which the visible effect of farmyard manure has continued for a long time, there has been previously a continuous application of the manure every year for a considerable number of years; by thus supplying more than the soil can destroy a substantial residue is accumulated. We have equally seen, in other instances, that the application of nitrogenous manure once in a rotation has its effect exhausted before the rotation is concluded. With any considerable increase in the quantity of farmyard manure applied its residual effect will increase in a still greater proportion; a double dressing of manure should give more than a double after effect where the circumstances of the case admit of the effect being shown. All these points must be taken into account in any attempt to value the unexhausted residue of organic manures.

VALUATION OF RESIDUES IN POOR AND RICH SOILS.

The facts I have brought before you lead, I think, distinctly to the conclusion that a different scale of valuation should be employed when dealing with land of very different quality, or receiving very different quantities of manure. We may conveniently classify farms for our present purpose as (1) those whose actual fertility is distinctly below the average; (2) those in a condition of average fertility; (3) those in which very liberal manuring is practised.

The first-named class will include those farm lands the natural fertility of which is very low, and which yield remunerative crops only when the soil is systematically supplied with plant food by means of manures, or the organic residues of fodder crops. It will also occasionally include land of naturally fair quality, which by a long course of exhaustive treatment has reached a low state of fertility; of such land we have had an example in that part of the rotation field at Rothamsted from which the whole of the crops have been removed for many years without the application of any nitrogenous manure. On the land in this class everything which makes either for the improvement or deterioration of the soil produces its largest effect. It is on such soil that the landlord must be most particular that roots and hay are not sold without full compensation being made. On such soils the referee may employ, without hesitation, his highest scale of valuation. All manures, indeed, produce their greatest effect when the land is very deficient in those substances which the manure supplies. Not only then is it for the general good of the country that encouragement should be given to every judicious effort to improve the fertility of poor land; it is also a fact, to which there are few exceptions,[1] that any residues of manure remaining in such land will yield a greater return to the next tenant than in the case of a rich soil.

The second class of farms includes the majority of those in this country. They consist of land which, when well cultivated and kept clean, may yield remunerative crops without much expenditure in purchased foods or manures, but which will yield larger, but still remunerative, crops under a higher condition of farming. It is not unusual to see farms standing side by side, and having the same quality of soil, which, nevertheless, exhibit a great variety in condition according to the style of farming adopted. The valuation of the residues of manures, in the case of farms in this class, will exercise to the full all the skill which the valuer possesses. The compensation to be made to the retiring tenant must not be measured by the quantity or cost of the imported manures, but by the substantial benefit which they will confer on his successor; the scale of valuation will thus vary according to the circumstances of each case.

Our third class is that of farms on fair soil to which excessive quantities of manure have been applied, the land containing, in consequence, more manure than can be turned to profitable

---

[1] A soil must clearly have some retentive power to establish a claim to compensation. In the case of a coarse gravel, a referee is not likely to place a high value on manure residues.

account by the crops. Excessive quantities of manure do not necessarily mean large applications, though this is the most common cause of excess. Any application of manure to land that does not need it is excessive; the richness of a soil may thus determine the uselessness of the manure. On farms where large quantities of manures and cake have been habitually employed, a heavy claim for compensation is to be expected from the outgoing tenant; such a claim should receive a strict scrutiny, and payment should only be awarded for such residues as will certainly benefit his successor. Applications of phosphates and potash salts to soils already well provided with these substances, will be so slow in rendering a profitable return that no notice can be taken of them in a valuation. The application of rich cake-fed manures to arable land, already very fertile, will, as we have already seen, yield no better result to the succeeding tenant than if ordinary farmyard manure had been employed. On pasture the cake manure would, however, probably have a more permanent effect. One who farms highly may indeed truly claim that he has more than fully maintained the fertility of his land; but he has done this at a wasteful cost, and he must not expect to be repaid for his extravagant use of manures at the expense of the next tenant.

VALUATION OF OIL-CAKE.

Before closing this lecture, I have a few words to say as to the effect of various modes of employing oil-cake upon its value as a manure. Cake may be used directly as a manure for crops; or it may be eaten by sheep on the land; or it may be consumed by stock at the farm buildings, and the manure afterwards brought on to the land. This farmyard manure may also be prepared in several ways, in which more or less loss of its valuable constituents may occur. The practical value of the cake as a manure is very different under these varying conditions of use.

At Rothamsted, rape-cake in powder has been used as a manure in many of the field experiments. In the barley field it has been used continuously for forty-five years. We take as our illustration the average produce of the second twenty years, as by so doing we include the whole effect of the residues of the manure, and thus obtain a maximum result. The annual application of 1,000 lbs. of rape-cake per acre, with superphosphate, has yielded on an average 40 bushels of barley ; the cake supplied about 49 lbs. of nitrogen. During the same twenty years, the application of 275 lbs. of nitrate of soda, with superphosphate, has given an average produce of $42\frac{1}{4}$ bushels ; the nitrate supplied about 43 lbs. of nitrogen. Approximately, therefore, the comparative value of nitrogen in nitrate of soda and rape-cake for the production of barley is as 100 to 83.

As cake nitrifies rather slowly, there would be more loss from autumn drainage on the cake plot than on the nitrate ; the two manures should thus be more equal in effect when applied to crops the growth of which extended into the autumn months. This is actually the case, the Rothamsted field experiments with mangel wurzel showing a still better return from cake applied as manure. On an average of twenty years, the annual application of 2,000 lbs. of rape cake, with manures supplying phosphates, potash, soda, and magnesia, has produced 20 tons $4\frac{3}{4}$ cwts. of mangel roots ; while 550 lbs. of nitrate of soda, with the same manures supplying ash constituents, have yielded 17 tons $11\frac{1}{2}$ cwts. of roots. The weights of these two crops are almost exactly in the same proportion as the quantities of nitrogen which they supply ; according to the figures, therefore, the nitrogen in the two manures had very nearly the same value. We may add, however, that in good seasons the nitraté gives generally the larger crop, while in a dry summer the seed germinates much better on the rape-cake plot.

The trial of rape-cake at Woburn as a manure for wheat and barley has lasted seven years, and the conditions of the experiment have not been such as to enable the cake to yield its most profitable return. The cake has been applied as a top dressing—to the wheat about the end of January, and to the barley just after the corn is up. The dressing has been a large one, supplying 82 lbs. of nitrogen per acre. No provision has been made for the supply of ash constituents to the crop. The results furnish a striking illustration of the poor return yielded by organic manures under such conditions.

In the wheat experiments the average crops during seven

years, 1890–96, have been : From nitrate of soda, containing 41 lbs. of nitrogen, employed with ash constituent manures, 28·6 bushels; from rape-cake, containing 82 lbs. of nitrogen, 27·1 bushels; from farmyard manure made from 188 lbs. of nitrogen in food and litter, applied as a top dressing, 26·8 bushels.

In the barley experiments, with precisely similar manures, the return from the nitrate of soda was 41 bushels ; from the rape-cake, 37·4 bushels ; from the farmyard manure, 42·8 bushels. Both in the experiments with wheat and barley the rape-cake thus appeared as inferior in effect to one-half its equivalent in nitrate of soda. The comparison made is, however, distinctly unfair to the cake, owing to the unequal quantities of nitrogen and ash constituents supplied in the comparative experiments.[1]

We turn next to the results obtained by consuming cake on the land. The present rotation experiments at Woburn, already described (Table V.), furnish us with a comparison of the effects of the manure of cake-fed sheep with that given by a nearly corresponding dressing of nitrate of soda. In eleven annual experiments, the consumption of about $21\frac{1}{2}$ lbs. of nitrogen as decorticated cotton-cake by sheep feeding off turnips increased the following crop of barley by 3 bushels ; while, at the same time, the application of 20 lbs. of nitrogen as nitrate of soda increased the barley crop by 6·1 bushels. The nitrogen of cake consumed on the land had thus about half the manurial value of the nitrogen as nitrate of soda.

Woburn supplies us with trials of farmyard manure, made under the most favourable circumstances, from food and litter containing a known quantity of nitrogen. This manure has been continuously applied as a top dressing for twenty years to both wheat and barley. How does the nitrogen of food when converted with great care into farmyard manure compare with the nitrogen of nitrate of soda ? To obtain the best

---

[1] The produce with nitrate of soda alone, without superphosphate or potash salts, was during the seven years, for wheat 22·6 bushels, and for barley 30·4 bushels. To compare these crops with the produce from the rape-cake is as unfair to the nitrate as the comparison above is unfair to the cake. The cake in fact contained some ash constituents, and was applied to a plot containing residues of farmyard manure.

answer to this question, we take the average produce of the second ten years, 1887–96, of the dunged plots, so that the effect of the residues of the manure may be included in the result. The average produce of wheat on plot 11b, receiving each year the manure from 188 lbs. of nitrogen as food and litter, is during this period 27·8 bushels; while 41 lbs. of nitrogen as nitrate of soda, employed with phosphates and potash, have yielded during the same season 30·1 bushels. On the corresponding plots in the barley field, the dung has yielded 39·9 bushels, and the nitrate 41·1. In both these cases the nitrogen of the food when converted into manure produces less than one-quarter the effect of the nitrogen in the form of nitrate of soda. The farmyard manure in these experiments is favourably circumstanced, for being of high quality and well rotted, only a small quantity, 7 to 8 tons, is applied every year. Half the quantity of dung applied for ten years on plot 10b gave only 21·7 bushels of wheat, and 30·5 bushels of barley; there appears therefore to be no reason to regard the larger application of dung as excessive.

We may approach the same question in another way. On plot 11a, as already mentioned (p. 17), the manure furnished by 188 lbs. of nitrogen as food and litter was applied for five years (six in the case of the barley experiments), and during the rest of the twenty years the land was left unmanured. We have already calculated (p. 19) the quantity of corn produced by the residue of the farmyard manure during the latter unmanured period; we can add this subsequent yield to that given in the years when the manure was actually applied, and thus arrive at the maximum produce which the manure was capable of producing.

In the wheat experiment we have the manure from 940 lbs. of nitrogen in food and litter producing an increase of 24·5 bushels during the five years of its application, and an additional 25·6 bushels during the thirteen following years, after which the effect ceased. We thus have 940 lbs. of nitrogen giving an increased produce of 50·1 bushels, or 1,000 lbs. producing 53 bushels. On plot 6, receiving nitrate of soda and ash constituents, we have on an average of twenty years 1,000 lbs. of nitrogen producing 322 bushels. The nitrogen of the food when converted into farmyard manure had thus only 16 per cent. of the value of the nitrogen in nitrate of soda.

The barley experiment yields a better result. Here we have 1,128 lbs. of nitrogen as food and litter producing in twenty years 152 bushels of barley, or 135 bushels per 1,000 lbs. of nitrogen. On plot 6, the nitrate of soda yielded during the same years 427 bushels per 1,000 lbs. of nitrogen. The nitrogen of the food thus had 32 per cent. the value of the nitrogen of nitrate of soda.

In summing up these results let us confine ourselves to those obtained with one crop, namely, barley. When powdered cake is applied directly as a manure for barley, and is ploughed into the ground before sowing, the practical effect of the nitrogen it contains is about 80 per cent. of the effect of the same quantity of nitrogen applied as nitrate of soda. When the cake is consumed by sheep feeding off turnips, its effect on the following barley is about 46 per cent. of that of the same quantity of nitrogen as nitrate of soda applied directly to the barley. When cake and other foods are consumed by fattening bullocks in deep stalls or boxes, the manure left undisturbed till the feeding is completed, then clamped, and finally applied as a top dressing in a well-rotted condition, the return in barley is about 20 per cent. of that yielded by the nitrogen of nitrate of soda ; this return may rise to about 30 per cent. if the effect of the residue in fifteen successive years without manure is taken into the account.

Nitrate of soda contains about 350 lbs. of nitrogen per ton. At its present price of £7. 15s. per ton, a pound of nitrogen is worth 5·3 pence. A pound of nitrogen in oil-cake is thus worth as a manure for barley 4·2 pence if applied directly to the crop ; 2·4 pence if consumed by sheep on the land ; and one penny if given to fattening bullocks in boxes, and the manure applied to the land. We have no experiments showing the manuring effect of food consumed in an open yard, or in stables where much of the liquid portion of the manure runs to waste. The final manuring value of cake consumed under such unfavourable conditions will be very low, perhaps not more than one halfpenny per pound of nitrogen in the cake.

These values for nitrogen do not express the whole manuring value of the cake, which is to a less extent due to the phosphates and potash which it contains. The relative manuring value of the nitrogen and ash constituents in foods is well shown in Lawes and Gilbert's Table.[1] In box-feeding there should be practically no loss of ash constituents. If urine is lost, much potash will go with it. If the rotted manure is washed by rain, both potash and phosphates will more or less escape. ·

When cake manure is applied in moderate quantities to mangels, it will yield a better return and have a higher value than when applied to a cereal crop; a better return will also probably be found when the manure is applied to turnips, potatoes, and grass land, though in these cases no exact experiments are available.

We have hitherto spoken of the value of nitrogen in food employed in various ways; a wholly different question is the value of nitrogen in farmyard manure. In making this manure very considerable losses of nitrogen have taken place, these losses being apparently much larger than have usually been believed. The nitrogen in the manure finally obtained will clearly have a higher value than the one penny per pound at which we have reckoned the food contributing to it. While the experiments at Rothamsted, and elsewhere, provide many examples of the return in crops from the use of known quantities of farmyard manure, it is unfortunate that none of these experiments give any exact information as to the quality and composition of the farmyard manure used. The estimated value of the manure is clearly in many cases too high, very little account having been taken of the serious losses occurring during its preparation.

None can be more sensible than myself of the insufficient foundation on which many of the estimates I have given you have been based. I have endeavoured to bring before you some of what appear to be the best ascertained facts relating to the practical value of manure residues; these facts are few, but they have a greater practical value than the estimates and assumptions on which valuations have hitherto been largely based. I trust that, before many years have expired, more exact and extended investigations will have relegated my lecture to the domain of ancient history.

[1] *Jour. Roy. Agri. Society*, 1897, 698.

Spottiswoode & Co. Printers, New-street Square, London, E.C.